CHRISTMAS AT HOME
Just Gingerbread

© 2010 by Barbour Publishing, Inc.

Compiled by Conover Swofford.

ISBN 978-1-60260-973-0

All scripture quotations are taken from the King James Version of the Bible.

Published by Barbour Publishing, Inc., P.O. Box 719, Uhrichsville, Ohio 44683, www.barbourbooks.com

Our mission is to publish and distribute inspirational products offering exceptional value and biblical encouragement to the masses.

Member of the
Evangelical Christian
Publishers Association

Printed in China.

CHRISTMAS AT HOME
Just Gingerbread

BARBOUR
PUBLISHING

CONTENTS

MUFFINS AND CUPCAKES

I will honor Christmas in my heart
and try to keep it all the year.

CHARLES DICKENS

BANANA GINGERBREAD MUFFINS

1 (14 ounce) package gingerbread cake and cookie mix
1 cup mashed bananas (about 2 medium bananas)
¾ cup quick-cooking oats
2 large eggs, slightly beaten
1 teaspoon vanilla
¾ cup water

Preheat oven to 375 degrees. Grease bottoms only of 16 medium muffin cups with cooking spray or line with paper baking cups. Place all ingredients in large bowl. Whisk together until well blended. Divide batter evenly among the muffin cups. Bake 15 to 20 minutes or until a toothpick inserted in the center comes out clean. Immediately remove from the pan to a wire rack to cool slightly before serving.

GINGERBREAD CUPCAKES 1

1½ cups flour
2 teaspoons ginger
2 teaspoons cinnamon
¼ teaspoon nutmeg
½ teaspoon cloves
1½ cups butter, softened

1½ cups sugar
3 tablespoons molasses
4 large eggs at room
  temperature
1 teaspoon vanilla

Preheat oven to 350 degrees. Line standard muffin tins with paper liners. In a small bowl, sift together flour and spices. In a large bowl, with mixer on medium, cream together butter and sugar until pale and fluffy. Add molasses and beat until well mixed. Add eggs, beating until well blended. Add vanilla. Reduce speed to low. Gradually add flour mixture, beating until just combined. Divide batter evenly among lined cups, filling each ¾ full. Bake 25 minutes or until toothpick inserted in center comes out clean. Transfer to wire rack to cool 10 minutes. Turn out cupcakes onto rack and let cool completely. Cupcakes can be stored up to 2 days at room temperature or frozen up to 3 months in airtight containers.

CHOCOLATE GINGERBREAD CUPCAKES

1 teaspoon baking soda
⅔ cup boiling water
1¼ cups flour
½ cup unsweetened cocoa powder
¼ teaspoon salt
1 teaspoon ginger
¼ teaspoon nutmeg

5 tablespoons butter, softened
½ cup dark brown sugar, packed
1 large egg at room temperature
⅔ cup molasses

Preheat oven to 350 degrees. Line a standard muffin tin with baking papers. Put baking soda into boiling water. In another bowl, sift together flour, cocoa, and spices. With mixer on medium speed, cream butter and brown sugar until fluffy. Beat in egg. Add molasses and baking soda mixture. Reduce speed to low. Mix in flour mixture and beat until well blended. Batter will look lumpy. Divide batter among prepared muffin cups, filling each about halfway. Bake about 20 minutes or until cupcakes test done. Cool 15 minutes and then remove cupcakes from pan to wire rack to cool completely. Cupcakes can be stored up to 3 days at room temperature in airtight containers.

GINGERBREAD AND MOLASSES CUPCAKES

3 cups flour
2 teaspoons baking soda
1 teaspoon salt
2 teaspoons ginger
1½ cups sugar

⅔ cup molasses
2 large eggs
1 cup butter, melted
⅓ cup hot water

Preheat oven to 350 degrees. Line standard muffin tins with paper liners. In a small bowl, whisk together flour, baking soda, salt, and ginger. In a separate bowl, whisk sugar, molasses, and eggs until smooth. Whisk in melted butter and hot water. Stir in flour mixture until just blended. Divide batter evenly among lined cups, filling each about ¾ full. Bake about 20 minutes or until toothpick inserted in center comes out clean. Cool cupcakes completely in pan before removing. Cupcakes can be stored overnight at room temperature or frozen up to 2 months in airtight containers.

GINGER-CARAMEL CUPCAKES

Caramel:
⅓ cup plus 2 tablespoons water
¾ cup sugar

Batter:
1 cup flour
¾ teaspoon baking powder
¼ teaspoon baking soda
½ teaspoon ginger
¼ teaspoon cinnamon
¼ teaspoon salt

6 tablespoons butter, softened
⅓ cup sugar
1 egg
⅓ cup sour cream

Frosting:
6 tablespoons butter,
   softened
2½ to 3 cups powdered
   sugar, sifted

Caramel: Place ⅓ cup water near stove. In small saucepan over medium-high heat, heat sugar and 2 tablespoons water until sugar starts to dissolve, 3 to 4 minutes. Swirl pan constantly as mixture starts to turn golden. When mixture begins to smoke, turns amber-colored, and sugar is dissolved (1 to 2 minutes) remove from heat. Watch very carefully, because sugar mixture will turn quickly. Add ⅓ cup water in 3 additions to saucepan, holding pan at arm's length to avoid spattering; mixture is very hot. Stir until caramel is dissolved, returning to heat if needed. Pour into 1-cup glass measuring cup. Add water to equal ¾ cup if needed. Let stand until room temperature. Use ½ cup for batter and ½ cup for frosting.

Batter: Heat oven to 350 degrees. Line sixteen 2½-inch muffin cups with foil liners. Coat lightly with cooking spray. In a small bowl, stir together first six ingredients. In a large bowl, beat butter and sugar until fluffy, 1 minute. Beat in egg and sour cream.Fold in flour mixture and ½ cup cooled caramel mixture in 3 additions, beginning and ending with flour. Spoon into muffin cups. Bake 25 minutes or until wooden pick comes out clean. Cool in pan 5 minutes. Remove cupcakes from pans; cool completely on wire rack.

Frosting: Beat butter until smooth. Gradually beat in powdered sugar and remaining ¼ cup caramel mixture; beat 1 minute or until creamy. Frost cupcakes. Garnish with currants, grapes, and gooseberries if desired.

DID YOU KNOW?

The original word for gingerbread came from a Sanskrit word, *singabera*, meaning "root-shaped like a horn." Ginger has been grown in India and southern China for countless centuries. The ancient Chinese used it as a medicine.

GINGERBREAD CUPCAKES 2

4 cups sifted flour
1 teaspoon baking soda
1 teaspoon ginger
⅛ teaspoon salt
1 cup butter or margarine, softened
1 cup brown sugar, firmly packed

2 eggs, well beaten
1 cup molasses
1 tablespoon boiling water

Preheat oven to 350 degrees. Line 24 standard muffin tins with paper liners. In a small bowl, stir together flour, baking soda, ginger, and salt; set aside. In a large bowl, cream together butter and brown sugar until fluffy. Add eggs and beat until well blended. Add molasses and boiling water. Mix well. Gradually add the flour mixture, beating well after each addition until blended. Spoon batter into muffin tins until each is half full. Bake about 20 minutes or until toothpick inserted in center comes out clean. Cool cupcakes completely in pan before removing. Cupcakes can be stored overnight at room temperature or frozen up to 2 months in airtight containers.

GINGERBREAD MUFFINS AND FRUIT

½ vanilla bean, split
½ cup unsalted butter
1½ cups flour
½ cup sugar
2½ teaspoons baking powder
⅛ teaspoon salt
1 teaspoon ginger
½ teaspoon cinnamon
½ cup buttermilk
1 large egg
¼ cup roughly chopped strawberries (about 3 large berries)
¼ cup banana, roughly chopped
½ cup raspberries

Preheat oven to 350 degrees. Butter 2 mini-muffin tins. Scrape seeds from vanilla bean; place pod and seeds in a saucepan. Add butter; heat over low heat until melted. Set aside until cooled. Remove and discard pod. In bowl of electric mixer sift flour, sugar, baking powder, salt, ginger, and cinnamon. Add reserved melted butter, buttermilk, and egg; mix until just combined. Divide batter in half. Stir strawberries and bananas into half until just combined. Stir raspberries into remaining half of batter. Spoon batter into prepared pans all the way to the top. Bake until golden, 25 to 30 minutes. Remove from oven; set on wire rack until cool.

DID YOU KNOW?

Over the course of gingerbread's history, its form varied from location to location. In some places, gingerbread was a soft cake, while in others, it was a crisp, flat cookie; in still other places, the treat came as warm, thick squares of "bread," sometimes served with a pitcher of lemon sauce or cream. Gingerbread was sometimes light and sometimes dark, sometimes sweet and sometimes spicy. Almost always it was cut into shapes—men, women, stars, or animals—and colorfully decorated or dusted with sugar.

GINGERBREAD

Joy to the world! The Lord is come!
Isaac Watts

GINGERBREAD 1

1½ cups flour
2 teaspoons baking powder
¼ teaspoon baking soda
½ teaspoon salt
2 teaspoons ginger
1 teaspoon cinnamon

¼ teaspoon cloves
½ cup butter, softened
½ cup sugar
1 egg at room temperature
¼ cup molasses
¾ cup sour cream

Preheat oven to 350 degrees. Line the bottom of an 8x8-inch pan with waxed paper and grease the paper and sides of the pan. Sift all dry ingredients together 3 times and set aside. In a large bowl, cream butter and sugar until light and fluffy. Beat in egg. Blend well. Stir in molasses. Add dry ingredients. Blend well. Add sour cream. Mix only enough to blend. Pour into prepared pan. Bake 45 to 50 minutes. Cut into squares. Serve warm.

GINGERBREAD 2

2⅓ cups flour
⅓ cup sugar
1 cup molasses
¾ cup hot water
½ cup butter or margarine, softened
1 egg
1 teaspoon baking soda
1 teaspoon ginger
1 teaspoon cinnamon
¾ teaspoon salt

Preheat oven to 325 degrees. Grease and flour a 9x9-inch-square pan. Beat all ingredients in a large bowl with mixer on low speed for 30 seconds. Beat on medium speed 3 minutes. Pour into pan. Bake about 50 minutes or until toothpick inserted in center comes out clean.

WHOLE-WHEAT GINGERBREAD

1 cup whole-wheat flour
1 cup all-purpose flour
¼ cup sugar
1 cup molasses
¾ cup hot water
½ cup butter or margarine

1 egg
1 teaspoon baking soda
1 teaspoon ginger
1 teaspoon cinnamon
¾ teaspoon salt

Preheat oven to 325 degrees. Grease and flour a 9x9-inch square pan. Beat all ingredients in large bowl with mixer on low speed for 30 seconds. Beat on medium speed for 3 minutes. Pour into pan. Bake about 50 minutes or until toothpick inserted in center comes out clean.

MARMALADE GINGERBREAD

1 (14 ounce) package gingerbread mix
¾ cup orange juice
½ cup orange marmalade

Combine gingerbread mix, orange juice, and marmalade; blend according to package directions. Pour into greased 8x8-inch dish. Shield each corner with a triangle of foil; mold foil around dish. Cook over low heat 8 minutes and at medium-high heat 6 to 8 minutes, or until toothpick inserted near center comes out clean. Let stand 10 minutes. Store, covered, until ready to serve.

NUT GINGERBREAD

2 cups flour
1 teaspoon baking soda
½ teaspoon salt
1 teaspoon ginger
1½ cups dark brown sugar, packed
½ cup molasses
¼ cup butter or margarine, melted

1 large egg, beaten
1 cup milk
5 tablespoons pecans, chopped
1½ tablespoons dark brown sugar

Preheat oven to 350 degrees. Grease a 9x13-inch baking pan generously. In a medium bowl, sift together flour, baking soda, salt, and ginger. In a large bowl, combine 1½ cups brown sugar, molasses, butter, and egg, mixing well. Add the dry ingredients alternately with the milk; beat until well blended. Pour into pan. Sprinkle with the pecans and the 1½ tablespoons brown sugar. Bake 30 minutes. Serve warm.

DID YOU KNOW?

In medieval England, gingerbread became a fairground treat. Many fairs became known as "gingerbread fairs," and in England gingerbread was called "fairings"—a gift brought from a fair. Certain gingerbread shapes were connected with different seasons: buttons and flowers were common at Easter fairs, and animals and birds were popular at harvest fairs.

FLUFFY GINGERBREAD

2 cups flour
1½ teaspoons baking soda
1 teaspoon cinnamon
½ teaspoon cloves
2 teaspoons ginger
½ cup butter or margarine, softened

½ cup sugar
2 eggs
¾ cup light corn syrup
1 cup boiling water

Preheat oven to 375 degrees. Grease and flour a 9x13-inch baking pan. In a small bowl, mix all dry ingredients. In a large bowl, cream butter and sugar until fluffy; add eggs and blend well. Stir in syrup; then add the dry ingredients, beating well. Add boiling water; stirring thoroughly. Pour batter into prepared pan. Bake 15 minutes or until sides of gingerbread leave pan. Serve hot.

HOT WATER GINGERBREAD 1

1 cup molasses
½ cup boiling water
2¼ cups flour
1 teaspoon baking soda
1½ teaspoons ginger
½ teaspoon salt
3 tablespoons butter, melted

Preheat oven to 350 degrees. Grease and flour an 8x8-inch baking pan. In a large bowl, add water to molasses. In a separate bowl, mix dry ingredients. Add to water mixture. Blend well. Add butter and beat at medium speed until well blended. Bake 25 minutes. Remove from oven and let cool in pan completely.

SOUR CREAM GINGERBREAD 1

1 cup molasses
1 cup sour cream
2½ cups flour
1¾ teaspoons baking soda
2 teaspoons ginger
½ teaspoon salt
½ cup butter, melted

Preheat oven to 350 degrees. Grease and flour an 8x8-inch baking pan. In a large bowl, add molasses to sour cream. Mix well. In a separate bowl, mix and sift dry ingredients. Combine mixtures. Blend well. Add butter and beat at medium speed until well blended. Pour into pan. Bake 25 minutes. Remove from oven and let cool in pan completely.

SOFT MOLASSES GINGERBREAD

½ cup butter
1 cup molasses
1¾ teaspoons baking soda
½ cup sour cream
1 egg
2 cups flour
2 teaspoons ginger
½ teaspoon salt

Preheat oven to 350 degrees. Grease and flour an 8x8-inch baking pan. Put butter and molasses in saucepan and bring just to the boiling point over medium heat. Remove from heat. Pour into medium bowl. Add baking soda. Whisk vigorously. Add all other ingredients. Blend well. Pour into pan and bake 15 minutes. Remove from oven and let cool in pan.

CAMBRIDGE GINGERBREAD

½ cup butter
⅔ cup boiling water
1 cup molasses
1 egg
3 cups flour
1½ teaspoons baking soda

½ teaspoon salt
1 teaspoon cinnamon
1 teaspoon ginger
¼ teaspoon cloves

Preheat oven to 350 degrees. Grease and flour an 8x8-inch baking pan. In a large bowl, melt butter in water. Add molasses, egg, and dry ingredients. Bake 15 minutes. Remove from oven and let cool in pan.

SOFT SUGAR GINGERBREAD

2 eggs
1 cup sugar
1¾ cups flour
3 teaspoons baking powder
½ teaspoon salt
1½ teaspoons ginger
⅔ cup cream

Preheat oven to 350 degrees. Grease and flour an 8x8-inch baking pan. In a large bowl, beat eggs until light. Add sugar gradually and beat until well blended. In a separate bowl, mix and sift dry ingredients. Add to eggs and sugar mixture alternately with cream. Blend well. Pour into pan. Bake 30 minutes. Remove from oven and let cool in pan.

DID YOU KNOW?

By the fifteenth century, ginger and gingerbread were well known in England. Ginger was the second most highly traded spice after pepper in medieval times. Throughout the sixteenth, seventeenth, and eighteenth centuries, gingerbread grew more and more fancy. Queen Elizabeth I hired a special artist-baker, whose only job was to create gingerbread lords and ladies in the images of her guests and courtiers to amuse and flatter them. Gingerbread "honors" were popular in other parts of Europe, too. When Peter the Great of Russia was born, his father's friends sent him dozens of huge gingerbread creations. One of the largest was the coat of arms of Moscow, complete with the Kremlin's turrets.

GOSSAMER GINGERBREAD

½ cup butter, softened
1 cup sugar
1 egg
½ cup milk
1¾ cups flour
3 teaspoons baking powder
1 teaspoon ginger

Preheat oven to 350 degrees. Grease and flour a 9x13-inch baking pan. In a large bowl, cream butter and sugar. Gradually beat in egg. Add milk and all dry ingredients. Mix well. Pour into pan. Bake 15 minutes. Remove from oven and cool in pan.

FAIRY GINGERBREAD 1

½ cup butter, softened
1 cup light brown sugar, packed
½ cup milk
1¾ cups bread flour
2 teaspoons ginger

Preheat oven to 350 degrees. Grease and flour a 9x13-inch baking pan. In a large bowl, cream butter and brown sugar. Add milk and blend well. Add flour and ginger. Spread evenly in baking pan. Bake 15 minutes. Remove from oven and cool in pan.

HARD SUGAR GINGERBREAD

¾ cup butter, softened
1½ cups sugar
¾ cup milk
5 cups flour
1½ teaspoons baking powder
1½ teaspoons salt
1½ teaspoons ginger

Preheat oven to 350 degrees. Grease and flour a 9x13-inch baking pan. Put all ingredients in large bowl. Mix well. Pour evenly in pan. Bake 15 minutes. Remove from oven and cool in pan.

MAMA'S GINGERBREAD

1 cup dark brown sugar
½ cup butter, softened
4 eggs
¾ cup molasses
2 teaspoons ginger
1 teaspoon baking soda
½ teaspoon cinnamon

½ teaspoon nutmeg
½ teaspoon allspice
½ teaspoon salt
2⅓ cups flour

Preheat oven to 350 degrees. Grease and flour a 9x13-inch baking pan. In a large bowl, mix all ingredients except flour. Blend well. Add flour. Mix until completely blended. Pour into prepared pan. Bake 30 minutes. Remove from oven. Serve warm.

STICKY GINGERBREAD

1⅔ cups self-rising flour
1½ teaspoons ginger
½ cup butter, softened
¾ cup molasses
2 large eggs
1 cup orange marmalade
½ cup golden raisins
½ cup chopped crystallized ginger (about 2 ounces)

Preheat oven to 325 degrees. Butter and flour a 9x9-inch metal baking pan; line bottom with waxed paper. In a small bowl, sift flour and ginger together. In a large bowl, beat butter until fluffy. Beat in molasses. Beat in flour mixture in 3 additions alternately with eggs, one egg at a time. Beat in marmalade, then raisins and ginger. Pour into baking pan. Bake about 38 minutes. Cool cake completely in pan on rack.

GINGERBREAD 3

1 cup butter, softened
½ cup sugar
2 eggs
1 cup molasses
1 teaspoon cinnamon
1½ teaspoons ginger
½ teaspoon salt

1 teaspoon baking soda
1 cup boiling water
3 cups flour
1 teaspoon baking powder
1 cup golden raisins

Preheat oven to 350 degrees. Grease a 3-quart oblong baking pan. In a large bowl, cream the butter and sugar. Add eggs, mixing well. Add the molasses, cinnamon, ginger, and salt; mix well. Dissolve the baking soda in the boiling water. Add to the creamed mixture. Sift in the flour and the baking powder. Mix well. Stir in the raisins. Pour mixture into pan. Bake 40 minutes.

GINGERBREAD 4

2 cups flour
1 teaspoon ginger
¾ teaspoon baking soda
½ cup butter
1 cup brown sugar, firmly packed
1 cup molasses
½ cup milk
4 eggs

Preheat oven to 350 degrees. Butter and flour 2 round 9-inch cake pans. In a large bowl, combine dry ingredients. Melt butter in saucepan. Remove from heat. Add sugar, molasses, and milk to saucepan. Whisk together. Add eggs to saucepan. Whisk together. Pour mixture into bowl of dry ingredients. Blend well. Pour into cake pans, dividing the batter evenly between the two pans. Bake 1 hour or until done.

MORAYSHIRE GINGERBREAD

1 cup butter, softened
½ cup sugar
1 cup molasses
2 eggs
2 cups flour
1 teaspoon baking soda
1 teaspoon ginger

1 teaspoon allspice
¼ teaspoon cloves
⅛ teaspoon salt
½ cup ground almonds
½ cup golden raisins
½ cup sultanas

Preheat oven to 250 degrees. Grease and flour a 9x13-inch pan. In a large bowl, cream butter and sugar; add molasses and beat in eggs. In a separate bowl, stir together flour, baking soda, spices, and salt. Add ground almonds and raisins. Mix flour mixture with butter mixture. Blend well. Pour into pan. Bake 2 hours.

OATMEAL GINGERBREAD

½ cup butter, softened
2 tablespoons molasses
1 cup flour
1 cup brown sugar
½ cup oatmeal
¾ teaspoon baking soda
1 egg
¼ cup milk

Preheat oven to 350 degrees. Grease and flour a 9x13-inch pan. Line bottom with waxed paper. In a small saucepan, melt butter and molasses. In a large bowl, mix dry ingredients. Add butter mixture to dry ingredients. Blend well. Add egg and milk. Blend well. Pour into pan. Bake for 20 minutes. Let cool in pan completely before removing.

FAIRY GINGERBREAD 2

1 cup butter, softened
2 cups sugar
1 tablespoon ginger
1 cup milk
4 cups flour
1 teaspoon baking powder

Preheat oven to 350 degrees. Grease and flour a 9x13-inch pan. In a large bowl, beat butter to a cream and add sugar gradually, beating constantly. Add ginger and then milk. Finally add flour and baking powder. Pour into pan. Bake 15 minutes or until golden brown.

MAPLE SYRUP GINGERBREAD

1 cup maple syrup
1 cup sour cream
2 eggs, well beaten
2½ cups flour

1¾ teaspoons baking soda
1½ teaspoons ginger
¼ teaspoon salt
4 tablespoons butter, melted

Preheat oven to 350 degrees. Grease a 9x13-inch pan. In a large bowl, combine maple syrup, sour cream, and eggs. Blend well. In a separate bowl, sift all the dry ingredients and stir into the liquid, beating well. Add butter and beat thoroughly. Pour into pan. Bake 30 minutes. Let cool completely in pan before removing.

BOSTON GINGERBREAD

1 cup sour milk
1 cup molasses
2¼ cups flour
1¾ teaspoons baking soda
2 teaspoons ginger
½ teaspoon salt
½ cup butter, melted
1 egg, well beaten

Preheat oven to 350 degrees. Grease an 8x8-inch pan. In a large bowl, mix milk and molasses. In a separate bowl, sift together flour, soda, ginger, and salt. Sift again and combine with milk and molasses mixture. Add butter and egg and beat until the mixture is smooth and creamy. Pour into pan. Bake 30 minutes.

APPLE GINGERBREAD 1

6 tablespoons butter, softened
⅓ cup sugar
1 egg, beaten
½ cup molasses
1¾ cups flour
½ teaspoon baking soda

1 teaspoon cinnamon
½ teaspoon ginger
½ teaspoon salt
⅔ cup unsweetened
    applesauce

Preheat oven to 350 degrees. Grease an 8x8-inch pan. In a large bowl, cream together butter and sugar. Add egg and molasses; mix well. In a separate bowl, sift together 3 times flour, soda, cinnamon, ginger, and salt. Add to creamed mixture alternately with applesauce. Bake 45 minutes. Cool slightly.

SOFT GINGERBREAD 1

2 cups molasses
⅔ cup butter, softened
3 teaspoons baking soda
2 eggs, beaten
1 cup sour cream

4 cups flour
1 tablespoon ginger
1 tablespoon cinnamon
1 teaspoon salt

Preheat oven to 350 degrees. Grease an 8x8-inch pan. In a saucepan, combine molasses and butter. Heat to boiling. Add soda and beat hard. Add eggs and sour cream. In a large bowl, combine all dry ingredients. Add saucepan mixture to dry ingredients. Blend well. Pour into pan. Bake 15 minutes. Serve warm.

GINGERBREAD 5

Sift together and set aside:
2½ cups sifted flour
1 teaspoon baking soda
½ teaspoon baking powder
½ teaspoon salt
1 teaspoon cinnamon
1 teaspoon ginger
½ teaspoon nutmeg
¼ teaspoon cloves
¼ teaspoon allspice

Combine and set aside:
1 cup molasses
1 cup boiling water

Cream together:
½ cup butter, softened
½ cup sugar
1 egg

Preheat oven to 350 degrees. Grease a 9x9-inch cake pan. Combine all mixtures in large bowl. Blend well. Pour into pan. Bake 50 minutes. Cool. Remove from pan.

DID YOU KNOW?

Gingerbread came to North America from all parts of northern Europe with the settlers who brought with them the traditions of their families. American recipes usually called for fewer spices than their European counterparts; they often made use of ingredients that were available only regionally. For instance, maple syrup gingerbreads were made in New England, while in the South sorghum molasses was used.

THIN GINGERBREAD

2 cups flour
½ cup butter, softened
2 cups sugar
3 eggs
1 tablespoon ginger

Preheat oven to 350 degrees. Mix all ingredients until well blended. Roll out as thin as possible. Place on baking sheets. Bake 10 minutes.

FAVORITE GINGERBREAD

½ cup butter, softened
2 tablespoons sugar
1 egg
1 cup molasses
1 cup boiling water

2¼ cups flour
1 teaspoon baking soda
½ teaspoon salt
1 teaspoon ginger
1 teaspoon cinnamon

Preheat oven to 325 degrees. Grease and flour 9x9-inch pan. In a large bowl, mix thoroughly butter, sugar, and egg. Blend in molasses and water. In a separate bowl, sift together dry ingredients. Add to butter mixture. Blend thoroughly. Pour into pan. Bake 45 minutes. Cut into squares. Serve hot.

NEW ORLEANS GINGERBREAD

2 cups molasses
¼ cup sugar
1 cup shortening
3 teaspoons cinnamon
1 teaspoon cloves

1 teaspoon ginger
1 teaspoon salt
½ cup boiling water
2 teaspoons baking powder

Preheat oven to 350 degrees. Grease 2 baking sheets. Mix ingredients as listed then sift and mix with as much flour as is required to make dough that can be molded by the hands into flat "stage planks" about 6 inches long, 3 inches wide, and ½ inch thick. Set on cookie sheets two inches apart. Bake 10 to 12 minutes or until golden brown. Store in airtight containers.

WALNUT GINGERBREAD

1 cup brown sugar
½ cup butter, softened
½ cup molasses
1 cup boiling water
3½ cups flour
2 teaspoons baking soda

½ teaspoon ginger
½ teaspoon cinnamon
½ teaspoon cloves
2 eggs
¾ cup walnuts, chopped

Preheat oven to 350 degrees. Grease and flour a loaf pan. In a large bowl, cream sugar and butter. Add molasses and pour boiling water over mixture. Mix well. In a separate bowl, combine flour, soda, and spices. Add to molasses mixture and beat well. Add eggs one at a time and blend thoroughly. Stir in nuts. Pour into loaf pan. Bake 40 minutes.

SUGAR GINGERBREAD

1 cup butter, softened
2 cups sugar
6 eggs, well beaten
2 cups flour
2 tablespoons ginger

Preheat oven to 325 degrees. Grease two 8x8-inch pans. Mix all ingredients thoroughly. Pour into pans. Bake 40 minutes.

DID YOU KNOW?

In the 1700s, gingerbread "hornbooks" were used to teach children their letters. Hornbooks were in every classroom for hundreds of years. They consisted of flat boards with handles, with a sheet of paper pasted on each board; the paper held a simple lesson for a beginning student and was protected with a thin sheet of horn. The gingerbread version of this teaching device allowed students to eat each letter of the alphabet as they learned it. What a tasty way to reinforce learning!

MOLASSES GINGERBREAD

½ cup butter, softened
½ cup sugar
1 cup molasses
1 egg, beaten
2 cups flour
½ teaspoon salt

1½ teaspoons baking soda
1 teaspoon cinnamon
1 teaspoon ginger
½ teaspoon cloves
1 cup hot water

Preheat oven to 350 degrees. Grease a 9x13-inch pan. In a large bowl, mix butter, sugar, molasses, and egg. In a separate bowl, sift together dry ingredients. Add to butter mixture. Stir until smooth. Add hot water and stir until smooth. Pour into pan. Bake 35 minutes.

BUTTERMILK GINGERBREAD

1½ cups flour
½ teaspoon allspice
¼ teaspoon salt
½ teaspoon baking soda
½ teaspoon cinnamon
½ teaspoon ginger
½ cup butter, softened
½ cup sugar
1 egg
½ cup molasses
½ cup plus 2 tablespoons buttermilk

Line bottom of an 8x8-inch pan with waxed paper. Grease paper and sides of pan lightly. Preheat oven to 350 degrees 10 minutes before baking. (If glass baking dish is used, preheat oven to 325 degrees.) Sift flour, measure, and resift 3 times with allspice, salt, soda, cinnamon, and ginger. In a separate bowl, cream butter until smooth. Add sugar and egg and beat until smooth and fluffy. Add molasses and beat vigorously 2 minutes longer. Clean off beater and remove. Add flour mixture and buttermilk alternately in 3 or 4 portions, beginning and ending with flour and beating with wooden spoon after each until smooth. Turn batter into prepared pan. Bake 25 to 30 minutes. Cool in pan on cake rack 4 minutes, then turn out on rack, strip off paper quickly, and invert. Serve warm with whipped cream, applesauce, or melted marshmallows.

APPLE GINGERBREAD 2

3 apples peeled, cored, and sliced
Brown sugar
½ cup butter or margarine, melted
½ cup molasses
½ cup sugar
⅓ cup brown sugar, packed
1 egg
2 cups flour

1 teaspoon baking soda
1 teaspoon cinnamon
1 teaspoon ginger
½ teaspoon cloves
½ teaspoon salt
¼ teaspoon nutmeg
¾ cup hot tea

Preheat oven to 350 degrees. Grease a 9x9-inch baking pan. Arrange apples in bottom of pan; sprinkle with brown sugar and set aside. For gingerbread, combine butter, molasses, sugars, and egg in a mixing bowl; mix well. In separate bowl combine dry ingredients; add to sugar mixture alternately with hot tea. Mix well; pour over apples. Bake 45 to 50 minutes or until the cake tests done. Cool for 3 to 5 minutes. Loosen sides and invert onto a serving plate. Serve warm.

SOUR CREAM GINGERBREAD 2

½ cup butter, softened
1 cup brown sugar
⅔ cup light molasses
2 egg yolks
½ cup sour cream
1½ cups flour
1 teaspoon cinnamon

¼ teaspoon nutmeg
¼ teaspoon cloves
1 teaspoon baking soda
2 tablespoons hot water
2 egg whites, beaten
1 teaspoon ginger

Preheat oven to 350 degrees. Grease and flour an 8x11-inch pan. In a large bowl, cream butter and brown sugar until light and smooth. Add molasses, egg yolks, and sour cream. Sift flour with the spices and add to the butter mixture. Dissolve soda in the hot water and add it to the mixture. Fold in stiffly beaten egg whites last. Pour into prepared pan. Bake 25 to 30 minutes. When gingerbread shrinks from the sides of the pan or springs back from the touch of the finger, it is done. Delicious served hot with butter.

ORANGE GINGERBREAD

½ cup butter, softened
½ cup light brown sugar
½ cup light molasses
1 egg, beaten
Juice and grated rind of 1 orange

½ cup cold strong tea
1¾ cup pastry flour
¾ teaspoon baking soda
1 teaspoon ginger

Preheat oven to 350 degrees. Grease and flour an 8x11-inch pan. In a large bowl, cream butter and brown sugar until smooth, then add the molasses, egg, orange juice, and rind. Beat well. Add tea and flour sifted with soda and ginger. Pour into prepared pan. Bake 30 minutes.

MAME'S GINGERBREAD

¾ cup butter, softened
¾ cup brown sugar
¾ cup light molasses
2 eggs, beaten till light
2½ cups sifted flour

1 teaspoon ginger
1 teaspoon cloves
1 teaspoon cinnamon
2 teaspoons baking soda
1 cup boiling water

Preheat oven to 350 degrees. Grease and flour a 9x13-inch pan. In a large bowl, cream together butter and sugar; when smooth add molasses. Add eggs. In a separate bowl, sift flour with ginger, cloves, and cinnamon and add to egg mixture. Dissolve soda in hot liquid and add it to the batter. Pour into prepared pan. Bake 35 to 40 minutes.

EGGLESS GINGERBREAD

1 cup molasses
1 cup sour cream
2 teaspoons baking powder
2¼ cups sifted flour
2 teaspoons ginger
⅛ teaspoon salt
½ cup butter, melted

Preheat oven to 350 degrees. Grease and flour an 8x11-inch pan. In a large bowl, mix molasses with sour cream and baking powder. Sift flour with remaining dry ingredients and combine with the sour cream mixture. Add the melted butter last. Pour into prepared pan. Bake 35 minutes.

HOT WATER GINGERBREAD 2

1 cup flour
½ cup sugar
1 teaspoon salt
1 teaspoon ginger
½ teaspoon baking soda
1 egg
½ cup molasses

½ cup hot water
1 tablespoon butter, softened

Topping:
2 tablespoons sugar
2 teaspoons cinnamon

Preheat oven to 350 degrees. Grease an 8-inch-square baking pan. In a small bowl, combine flour, sugar, salt, ginger, and baking soda; set aside. In a mixing bowl, beat egg, molasses, water, and butter until smooth. Gradually add dry ingredients and beat for 1 minute. Pour into prepared pan. For topping, combine sugar and cinnamon; sprinkle evenly over gingerbread. Bake 25 minutes or until a wooden pick inserted near the center comes out clean. Cool completely before cutting. Top each square with whipped topping prior to serving.

DID YOU KNOW?

When the Grimm brothers collected volumes of German fairy tales, they found one about Hansel and Gretel, two children who, abandoned in the woods by destitute parents, discovered a house made of gingerbread and candies. "Nibble, nibble like a mouse," cackled the witch. "Who's that nibbling on my house?"

HADDON HALL GINGERBREAD

2¼ cups flour
1 egg
1 teaspoon baking soda
⅓ cup sugar
1 teaspoon ginger
1 cup dark molasses
1 teaspoon cinnamon
¾ cup hot water

¾ teaspoon salt
½ cup shortening

Filling:
1 (8 ounce) package cream
  cheese, softened
½ cup milk

Heat oven to 325 degrees. Grease and flour a 9-inch-square pan. Measure all ingredients into large mixer bowl. Blend 30 seconds on low speed, scraping bowl constantly. Beat 3 minutes on medium speed, scraping bowl constantly. Pour into pan. Bake 50 minutes or until wooden pick inserted in center comes out clean. For filling, beat cream cheese and milk until fluffy. Cut gingerbread into 12 pieces. Split each piece to make 2 layers. Fill layers with about ½ tablespoon of filling. Top pieces with remaining cream cheese mixture.

IOWA GINGERBREAD

2 teaspoons baking soda
1 cup hot coffee
1 teaspoon cinnamon
1 teaspoon cloves
½ cup butter, softened

2½ cups flour
1 cup molasses
1 cup raisins
1 teaspoon ginger
2 eggs, well beaten

Preheat oven to 375 degrees. Lightly grease a 9x13-inch baking pan. In a large bowl, dissolve baking soda in coffee. Add remaining ingredients and pour into a pan. Bake 30 to 40 minutes, until a fork inserted in middle comes out clean.

COUNTRY GINGERBREAD

1 cup molasses
1 cup buttermilk
2¼ cups flour
1¾ teaspoons baking powder

2 teaspoons ginger
½ teaspoon salt
1 egg, beaten
½ cup oil

Preheat oven to 350 degrees. Grease a 9x9-inch pan. In a large bowl, mix molasses and buttermilk. In a separate bowl, sift together flour, baking powder, ginger, and salt. Add to milk mixture. Add egg and oil. Beat until smooth and creamy. Pour into pan. Bake at 350 degrees about 30 minutes.

GRANDMOTHER'S GINGERBREAD

½ cup brown sugar
½ cup solid shortening
2 eggs
¼ cup molasses
1¼ cups sifted flour
¼ teaspoon salt

1 teaspoon baking soda
¼ teaspoon baking powder
1¼ teaspoons ginger
1 teaspoon cinnamon
¼ teaspoon ground cloves
½ cup hot water

Preheat oven to 350 degrees. Grease and flour a 9x9-inch baking pan. In a large bowl, combine brown sugar, shortening, eggs, and molasses; blend well. In a separate bowl, combine flour, salt, baking soda, baking powder, ginger, cinnamon, and cloves; gradually blend into molasses mixture. Blend in hot water; pour batter into pan. Bake 25 to 30 minutes. Serve warm with Citrus Fluff (see recipe on p. 69).

CITRUS FLUFF

1 egg
½ cup sugar
1 teaspoon orange peel, grated
1 teaspoon lemon peel, grated
2 tablespoons lemon juice
1 cup whipped cream

In a small saucepan, beat egg. Add sugar, grated orange peel, grated lemon peel, and lemon juice. Cook and stir over low heat until thickened, about 5 minutes. Cool thoroughly. Fold in whipped cream. Chill. Spoon onto warm squares of Grandmother's Gingerbread (see recipe on p. 68). Garnish with a twist of orange.

INVERNESS GINGERBREAD

1¼ cups flour
¼ cup fine oatmeal
1 cup butter, softened
½ cup whole milk
1¼ cups molasses
2 tablespoons green ginger
¼ cup candied lemon peel, cut into fine shreds

Preheat oven to 350 degrees. Grease a 9x13-inch pan. In a small bowl, mix the flour and oatmeal together. In a large bowl, cream butter. Beat in the flour mixture and milk alternately. Stir in molasses, then add ginger and lemon peel. Work into a light dough, turn into pan, and bake about 45 minutes.

SOFT GINGERBREAD 2

½ cup butter or shortening
1 cup sugar
2 eggs, well beaten
1 cup molasses
3 cups flour
2 teaspoons cinnamon
1 teaspoon cloves
1 teaspoon ginger
¼ teaspoon nutmeg
1 cup buttermilk
1 teaspoon baking soda, dissolved in ¼ cup boiling water

Preheat oven to 350 degrees. Generously grease a 9x13-inch pan. In a large bowl, cream butter and sugar; add eggs and molasses and mix well. In a separate bowl, sift flour and spices; add alternately with buttermilk to butter mixture. Stir in dissolved soda. Pour into pan and bake 30 minutes.

LAURA INGALLS WILDER'S GINGERBREAD

1 cup brown sugar
½ cup shortening
½ cup molasses
2 teaspoons baking soda
1 cup boiling water
3 cups flour
1 teaspoon ginger

1 teaspoon cinnamon
1 teaspoon allspice
1 teaspoon nutmeg
1 teaspoon cloves
½ teaspoon salt
2 eggs, beaten

Preheat oven to 350 degrees. In a large bowl, cream together brown sugar and shortening. Add molasses and mix well. Dissolve baking soda in boiling water; add to sugar mixture. In small bowl sift together flour and spices. Add dry ingredients to wet ingredients and mix well. Mix in eggs. Batter should be quite thin. Bake 30 minutes.

DID YOU KNOW?

In medieval England, if a fair honored a town's patron saint, the saint's image might be stamped into the gingerbread. If the fair was on a special market day, the cakes would be decorated with icing to look like men, animals, valentine hearts, or flowers. Sometimes the dough was simply cut into round "snaps." One English tradition was that unmarried women had to eat gingerbread "husbands" at the fair if they wanted to meet a real husband.

EDINBURGH GINGERBREAD

1 cup flour
1 teaspoon baking soda
1 teaspoon cinnamon
1 teaspoon cloves
1 teaspoon ginger
½ cup butter

2 tablespoons sugar
¼ cup molasses
2 eggs
½ cup raisins
¼ cup slivered almonds

Preheat oven to 350 degrees. Grease an 8x8-inch cake pan. Sift flour, soda, and spices into a large bowl. In a small saucepan over medium-high heat, combine the butter, sugar, and molasses and bring to a boil. In a small bowl, beat the eggs; pour molasses mixture over them, stirring vigorously. Add this mixture to dry ingredients and beat thoroughly. Pour into pan and bake 1 hour.

GINGERBREAD COOKIES

And she brought forth her firstborn son, and wrapped him in swaddling clothes, and laid him in a manger.

LUKE 2:7

CHRISTMAS GINGERBREAD COOKIES

¾ cup sugar
⅔ cup butter or margarine, softened
¼ cup orange juice
½ cup dark corn syrup
½ cup dark molasses
4½ cups flour
¾ cup whole-wheat flour

2 teaspoons ginger
1 teaspoon baking soda
1 teaspoon salt
½ teaspoon cloves
½ teaspoon nutmeg
½ teaspoon allspice

In a large bowl, cream sugar and butter. Blend in orange juice, corn syrup, and molasses. Combine flours, ginger, baking soda, salt, cloves, nutmeg, and allspice. Add to creamed mixture; mix well. Chill 3 to 4 hours or overnight. Roll a portion of the dough on a lightly floured surface to ¼-inch thickness. Cut into desired shapes. Place 2 inches apart on greased baking sheets. Repeat with remaining dough. Bake at 350 degrees for 12 to 14 minutes. Cookies will be soft and chewy if baked 12 minutes—crunchy if baked 14 minutes.

GRANNY'S GINGERBREAD COOKIES

1 cup butter or margarine, softened
1½ cups sugar
1 egg, lightly beaten
2 tablespoons light corn syrup
2 tablespoons orange peel, grated
1 tablespoon cold water

3¼ cups flour
2 teaspoons baking soda
2 teaspoons cinnamon
1 teaspoon ginger
½ teaspoon cloves

In a large bowl, cream butter and sugar. Add egg, corn syrup, orange peel, and cold water. In a separate bowl, combine flour, baking soda, cinnamon, ginger, and cloves; add to creamed mixture and mix well. Chill for at least 1 hour. Preheat oven to 375 degrees. On a lightly floured surface, roll dough, a portion at a time, to ⅛-inch thickness. Cut into desired shapes. Place on greased baking sheets. Decorate as desired. Bake 6 to 8 minutes or until lightly browned.

GINGER CRISPS

½ cup light molasses
½ cup butter or margarine, softened
½ cup sugar
1 tablespoon vinegar

2 cups flour
1 teaspoon cinnamon
½ teaspoon ginger
1½ teaspoons baking soda

In a 1-quart saucepan, combine molasses, butter, sugar, and vinegar. Stir well and place over moderate heat; boil gently exactly 3 minutes, stirring constantly. Remove from heat and cool. Meanwhile, sift flour, measure, resift 3 times with the rest of the dry ingredients. Add dry ingredients to cooled molasses mixture in 2 or 3 portions, mixing after each until smooth. Shape dough into a ball; wrap in waxed paper and chill overnight or for several hours. Preheat oven to 375 degrees. Grease baking sheets. Roll dough out thin on a lightly floured surface. Cut with a 2-inch round cutter. Place 1½ inches apart on prepared baking sheet. Bake about 7 minutes or until a rich brown. Immediately remove from pan to cake rack to cool.

GINGER CREAM COOKIES

½ cup shortening
1 cup sugar
1 egg
1 cup molasses
4 cups flour
2 teaspoons ginger

2 teaspoons baking soda
1 teaspoon cloves
1 teaspoon cinnamon
1 teaspoon nutmeg
½ teaspoon salt
1 cup hot water

Preheat oven to 400 degrees. Grease baking sheets. In a large bowl, cream shortening and sugar; blend in egg and molasses. In a separate bowl, sift together dry ingredients and add alternately to shortening mixture with hot water. Drop by teaspoonfuls onto baking sheets and bake about 8 minutes.

THREE GINGER COOKIES

½ cup dark brown sugar, packed
½ cup unsalted butter, softened
1 tablespoon fresh ginger root
½ teaspoon vanilla
1 tablespoon ground ginger
3 to 4 pieces crystallized ginger, cut into small pieces
1¼ cups flour
¼ teaspoon baking soda
Pinch salt
Slivers crystallized ginger

In a large bowl, cream sugar, butter, and fresh ginger root until smooth. Add vanilla. In a separate bowl, mix ground ginger, crystallized ginger, flour, baking soda, and salt together. Add dry ingredients to butter mixture. Form dough into log about 2 inches square. Wrap in plastic and chill until firm (about 1 hour). Preheat oven to 350 degrees. Slice log into $\frac{1}{4}$-inch slices and press a sliver of crystallized ginger into the center of each slice. Bake 8 to 10 minutes, until light golden.

CENTURY GINGER SNAPS

1 cup molasses
¼ cup shortening
Pinch salt
⅔ teaspoon baking soda
1 teaspoon ginger
1 to 2 cups flour

Preheat oven to 400 degrees. In a saucepan over medium-high heat, bring molasses to a boil. Add shortening, salt, baking soda, and ginger. Allow to cool. Mix in enough flour to roll very thin, and bake 8 minutes.

GINGERBREAD SNICKERDOODLES

1 cup sugar, divided
½ cup brown sugar
½ cup butter, softened
½ cup margarine, softened
1 egg
⅓ cup molasses

2¼ cups flour, divided
2 teaspoons ginger
½ teaspoon nutmeg
2 teaspoons baking soda
½ teaspoon salt
1¼ teaspoons cinnamon

In a large bowl, cream ½ cup sugar with brown sugar, butter, and margarine until light and fluffy. Add egg and continue beating until well blended. Add molasses. Stir together. In a separate bowl, sift together flour, ginger, nutmeg, baking soda, salt, and 1 teaspoon cinnamon; stir into butter mixture. Refrigerate 30 minutes. Preheat oven to 325 degrees. Grease baking sheets. Place remaining ½ cup sugar in a shallow dish. Add ¼ teaspoon cinnamon. Mix well. Roll tablespoonfuls of the dough into balls, then roll the balls in the cinnamon-sugar mixture to coat. Place the cookie balls 2 inches apart on baking sheets. Flatten slightly with palm of hand. Bake 12 to 15 minutes. Let stand 5 minutes before removing to wire rack to cool.

GINGERBREAD PEOPLE

1½ cups dark molasses
1 cup brown sugar
⅔ cup cold water
½ cup shortening
7 cups flour
2 teaspoons baking soda

1 teaspoon salt
1 teaspoon allspice
2 teaspoons ginger
1 teaspoon cloves
1 teaspoon cinnamon

In a large bowl, mix molasses, brown sugar, water, and shortening. Mix in remaining ingredients. Cover and refrigerate at least 2 hours. Preheat oven to 350 degrees. Lightly grease baking sheets. Roll dough ¼-inch thick on floured board. Cut into desired shapes. Place 2 inches apart on baking sheets. Bake 10 to 12 minutes. Cool.

OLD-FASHIONED GINGERBREAD MEN

1 cup brown sugar, packed	1 teaspoon salt
3 eggs	3 cups flour
1¼ cups molasses	1 teaspoon cinnamon
1 cup butter, softened	1 teaspoon ginger
1 tablespoon baking soda	1 teaspoon allspice

In a large bowl, combine all ingredients. Beat well. Stir in 3 cups flour to make stiff dough. Divide dough in half and wrap in plastic; refrigerate at least 3 hours (or up to 1 week). Preheat oven to 350 degrees. Lightly grease baking sheets. Roll dough to ⅛-inch thickness. Cut into desired shapes. Place on baking sheets. Bake 12 minutes.

GINGERBREAD MEN

¼ cup butter, softened
½ cup brown sugar
½ cup molasses
3½ cups flour
1 teaspoon baking soda

¼ teaspoon cloves
½ teaspoon cinnamon
2 teaspoons ginger
½ teaspoon salt
¼ cup water

Preheat oven to 350 degrees. Grease baking sheets. In a large bowl, cream together butter and brown sugar. Beat in molasses. Sift together flour, baking soda, cloves, cinnamon, ginger, and salt. Add sifted ingredients to butter mixture. Stir in water. Roll dough to ¼-inch thickness. Cut into desired shapes and place on baking sheets. Bake 10 minutes.

GIANT GINGERBREAD KIDS

½ cup sugar
½ cup shortening
½ cup dark molasses
¼ cup water
¾ teaspoon salt

¾ teaspoon ginger
½ teaspoon baking soda
¼ teaspoon allspice
2½ cups flour

In a large bowl, beat sugar, shortening, molasses, and water on low speed until blended. Beat on medium speed 1 minute. Stir in remaining ingredients. Cover and refrigerate until chilled, 1 to 2 hours. Preheat oven to 375 degrees. Lightly grease baking sheet. Roll dough to ¼-inch thickness. Use 8-inch gingerbread man cookie cutter. Place cookies on baking sheet. Bake 8 to 10 minutes. Cool.

MOLASSES GINGERBREAD COOKIES

1½ cups flour
2 teaspoons ginger
1 teaspoon baking soda
¼ teaspoon baking powder
½ teaspoon cinnamon
¼ teaspoon cloves

¼ teaspoon salt
½ cup butter, softened
¾ cup brown sugar
¼ cup molasses
1 large egg

In a medium bowl, sift together all dry ingredients. In a separate bowl, beat together all wet ingredients, including egg. Add dry mixture to wet mixture and blend well. Wrap dough in plastic and chill overnight. Preheat oven to 375 degrees. Grease baking sheets. Make 1-inch balls of dough. Place 2 inches apart on baking sheets. Bake 12 to 14 minutes.

GINGERBREAD NUTBALLS

½ cup sugar
½ cup brown sugar
½ cup butter, softened
½ cup margarine, softened
1 egg
⅓ cup molasses
2¼ cups flour

2 teaspoons ginger
½ teaspoon nutmeg
1 teaspoon cinnamon
2 teaspoons baking soda
½ teaspoon salt
1 cup nuts, finely crushed

In a large bowl, cream sugars, butter, and margarine until light and fluffy. Add egg and continue beating until blended well. Add molasses. Stir together. In a separate bowl, sift together dry ingredients then stir into the butter mixture. Refrigerate for 30 minutes. Preheat oven to 325 degrees. Grease baking sheets. Place crushed nuts in a shallow dish. Roll tablespoonfuls of the dough into balls; then roll the balls in the crushed nuts to coat. Place the cookie balls 2 inches apart on baking sheets. Bake 12 to 15 minutes. Let stand 5 minutes before removing to wire rack to cool.

GINGERBREAD MARMALADE THUMBPRINTS

2 tablespoons orange marmalade
1 tablespoon pecans, finely chopped
2½ cups flour
½ teaspoon nutmeg
½ teaspoon ginger
½ teaspoon cinnamon

½ teaspoon salt
1 cup butter
⅔ cup sugar
1 large egg
2 teaspoons vanilla

Preheat oven to 375 degrees. In a small bowl, combine marmalade and pecans; set aside. In a medium bowl, combine flour, spices, and salt; set aside. In a large bowl, beat butter and sugar until light and fluffy. Beat in egg and vanilla. Reduce mixer speed to low; gradually beat in flour mixture until well mixed. Measure a tablespoon of dough and shape into a ball. Make a total of 36 balls. Place balls 2 inches apart on ungreased large baking sheet. With thumb, make an indentation in top of each ball of dough. Spoon about ¼ teaspoon marmalade mixture into each indentation. Bake 10 to 12 minutes, until edges are lightly browned. Cool cookies 2 minutes on baking sheets, then transfer to wire racks and cool completely. Store in airtight container.

GINGERBREAD APPLE COOKIES

½ cup butter, softened
1 cup brown sugar, packed
½ cup unsweetened applesauce
1 large egg

1½ teaspoons ginger
1 teaspoon baking soda
½ teaspoon salt
2¾ cups flour

Preheat oven to 350 degrees. In a large bowl, beat butter and sugar until fluffy. Beat in remaining ingredients. Drop by teaspoonfuls 2 inches apart on ungreased baking sheets. Bake 10 to 12 minutes.

GINGERBREAD COOKIE CUTOUTS

5½ cups flour
1 teaspoon baking soda
1½ teaspoons salt
1 tablespoon ginger
1 tablespoon cinnamon
1½ teaspoons cloves

1 teaspoon nutmeg
1 cup butter, softened
1 cup brown sugar
2 large eggs
1½ cups molasses

In a small bowl, whisk together flour, baking soda, salt, and spices. In a large bowl, cream butter and brown sugar with an electric mixer on medium-high speed until pale and fluffy. Add eggs and molasses and beat to combine. Reduce speed to low. Gradually add flour mixture, beating until just combined. Divide dough into thirds. Flatten each piece into a disk and wrap in plastic. Refrigerate until firm, at least 1 hour. Preheat oven to 350 degrees. Lightly grease baking sheets. Roll out to ¼-inch thickness and cut with cookie cutters. Place on baking sheets. Bake 8 to 10 minutes.

GINGERBREAD DROP COOKIES

2 cups flour
1 cup sugar
½ cup butter
1 egg
2 tablespoons milk
1 teaspoon baking powder
¼ cup molasses
1 teaspoon ginger

Preheat oven to 375 degrees. Lightly grease baking sheets. Mix all ingredients.
Drop by teaspoonfuls onto baking sheets. Bake 8 minutes.

GINGIES

½ cup shortening
1 cup brown sugar
1½ cups molasses
⅔ cup cold water
6 cups flour
2 teaspoons baking soda

1 teaspoon salt
1 teaspoon allspice
1 teaspoon ginger
1 teaspoon cloves
1 teaspoon cinnamon

In a large bowl, mix shortening, brown sugar, and molasses thoroughly. Stir in water. In a separate bowl, blend all dry ingredients together. Stir into shortening mixture. Chill. Preheat oven to 350 degrees. Lightly grease baking sheets. Roll dough to ½-inch thickness. Cut with round cookie cutter. Place on baking sheets. Bake 15 minutes.

DID YOU KNOW?

In the 1700s and 1800s, autumn fairs in Germany sold gingerbread hearts, decorated with white and colored icing and tied with ribbons. In the city of Nuremberg, gingerbread was not baked in the home but was made exclusively by a guild of master bakers. Nuremberg became known as the "gingerbread capital" of the world, and many gingerbread craftsmen were attracted to the town. Sculptors, painters, woodcarvers, and goldsmiths all contributed to the most beautiful gingerbread cakes in Europe. They carved wooden molds and decorated the gingerbread with frosting or gold paint. Intricate hearts, angels, and wreaths were sold at fairs, carnivals, and markets.

CRISP GINGERBREAD COOKIES

1 cup molasses
½ cup shortening
1 teaspoon baking soda
2¼ cups flour
1¾ teaspoons baking powder
1 teaspoon salt
1½ teaspoons ginger

In a saucepan, heat molasses to boiling point. Remove from heat. Stir in shortening and soda. Add all other ingredients. Mix well. Chill dough at least 1 hour. Preheat oven to 350 degrees. Lightly grease baking sheets. Roll dough to ⅛-inch thickness. Cut into desired shapes. Place on baking sheets. Bake 5 to 7 minutes.

MORAVIAN GINGERBREAD COOKIES

½ cup molasses
3 tablespoons soft shortening
2 tablespoons brown sugar
1¼ cups flour
½ teaspoon salt

½ teaspoon baking soda
¼ teaspoon ginger
¼ teaspoon cinnamon
¼ teaspoon cloves

In a large bowl, mix molasses, shortening, and brown sugar thoroughly. In a separate bowl, blend all dry ingredients. Stir into molasses mixture. Chill 4 hours. Preheat oven to 375 degrees. Grease baking sheets. Roll dough to ⅛-inch thickness. Cut into desired shapes. Place on baking sheets. Bake 5 to 6 minutes.

SUGAR-FREE GINGERBREAD DROP COOKIES

2 cups flour
1 cup brown sugar substitute
½ cup butter
1 egg
2 tablespoons milk
1 teaspoon baking powder
¼ cup molasses
1 teaspoon ginger

Preheat oven to 375 degrees. Mix all ingredients. Drop by teaspoonfuls onto lightly greased cookie sheets. Bake 8 minutes.

SUGAR-FREE GINGERBREAD CUTOUT COOKIES

1½ cups dark molasses
1 cup brown sugar substitute
⅔ cup cold water
½ cup shortening
7 cups flour
2 teaspoons baking soda

1 teaspoon salt
1 teaspoon allspice
2 teaspoons ginger
1 teaspoon cloves
1 teaspoon cinnamon

In a large bowl, mix molasses, brown sugar substitute, water, and shortening. Mix in remaining ingredients. Cover and refrigerate at least 2 hours. Preheat oven to 350 degrees. Lightly grease baking sheets. Roll dough ¼ inch thick on floured board. Cut into desired shapes. Place 2 inches apart on baking sheets. Bake 10 to 12 minutes. Cool.

OLD-FASHIONED SUGAR-FREE
GINGERBREAD COOKIES

8 cups flour
½ teaspoon salt
4 teaspoons baking soda
1 tablespoon ginger
1 teaspoon cinnamon

3 cups molasses
1 cup shortening, melted
½ cup butter
10 tablespoons boiling water

In a bowl, sift together dry ingredients. In a separate bowl, combine molasses, shortening, butter, and boiling water. To this mixture add 4 cups dry ingredients; blend well. Add remaining dry ingredients. Chill 1 hour. Preheat oven to 425 degrees. Roll dough and cut into desired shapes. Place on baking sheets. Bake 15 minutes.

SWEDISH GINGERBREAD COOKIES

1 cup butter or margarine, softened	3¼ cups sifted flour
1½ cups sugar	2 teaspoons baking soda
1 egg	2 teaspoons cinnamon
1½ tablespoons orange peel, grated	1 teaspoon ginger
2 tablespoons dark corn syrup	½ teaspoon cloves
1 tablespoon water	Blanched almonds

In a large bowl, thoroughly cream butter and sugar. Add egg and beat till light and fluffy. Add orange peel, corn syrup, and water; mix well. In a separate bowl, sift together dry ingredients; stir into creamed mixture. Chill dough thoroughly. Preheat oven to 375 degrees. On lightly floured surface, roll dough to ⅛-inch thickness. (For a sparkly look, sprinkle rolled dough with sugar, then press it in lightly with a rolling pin.) Cut into desired shapes with floured cookie cutter. Place 1 inch apart on ungreased baking sheet. Top each cookie with blanched almond half. Bake 8 to 10 minutes. Cool on rack.

GUNNING GINGERBREAD COOKIES

1 teaspoon salt
1 teaspoon baking soda
1½ teaspoons ginger
½ cup shortening
⅔ cup sugar

1 cup unsulphured molasses
1 tablespoon cider vinegar
3 tablespoons water
3 cups sifted flour

Preheat oven to 350 degrees. Lightly grease baking sheets. In a large bowl, mix together salt, baking soda, ginger, and shortening. Gradually add sugar and molasses. In a small bowl, combine vinegar and water; add to the mixture alternately with flour. Drop dough by tablespoonfuls, 2 inches apart, onto baking sheets. Bake 8 to 10 minutes.

OTHER GINGERBREAD SPECIALTIES

The King of glory sends his Son,
To make his entrance on this earth;
Behold the midnight bright as noon,
And heav'nly hosts declare his birth!

ISAAC WATTS

GINGERBREAD WASSAIL

1 large orange with peel cut into 8 pieces
1 large lemon with peel cut into 8 pieces
2 cinnamon sticks broken into small pieces
¼ teaspoon allspice
¼ teaspoon ginger
32 ounces all-natural apple juice

Place all ingredients in slow cooker. Heat on low until heated through—about 1½ hours. Serve warm.

GINGERBREAD CRUST

1 cup sugar
½ cup brown sugar
½ cup butter, softened
½ cup margarine, softened
1 egg
⅓ cup molasses

2¼ cups flour
2 teaspoons ginger
½ teaspoon nutmeg
1 teaspoon cinnamon
2 teaspoons baking soda
½ teaspoon salt

In a large bowl, mix all ingredients thoroughly. Refrigerate 1 hour. Roll out to ⅛-inch thickness. Line two 8-inch round pie plates with dough. Fill with pie filling and bake according to pie directions. Makes a great crust for pumpkin pie.

GINGER-PIGNOLI SHORTBREAD

¾ cup powdered sugar
⅓ cup crystallized ginger
½ teaspoon salt
2¼ cups flour

1 cup chilled unsalted
  butter, cut into pats
6 tablespoons pine nuts

Preheat oven to 350 degrees. Coat two 9-inch round baking pans with nonstick cooking spray. Combine powdered sugar, crystallized ginger, and salt in food processor. Whirl until ginger is finely chopped, about 10 seconds. Add flour and mix until combined. Add butter and pulse until the butter is finely chopped. Continue to mix until dough starts to come together. Crumble mixture into prepared pans, dividing evenly. Press mixture evenly over bottoms of pans; press flat bottom of glass measure on top of dough to compact and level dough. Sprinkle on pine nuts and pat lightly into dough. Bake 20 to 25 minutes or until shortbread is golden. Cool in pans on wire racks for 10 minutes. While still warm, cut into 12 equal wedges. Store wedges in airtight container at room temperature for up to 2 weeks.

EASY GINGERBREAD PANCAKES

1 tablespoon cinnamon
1 tablespoon ginger
4 cups buttermilk pancake dry mix
2⅓ cups water mixed with ½ cup molasses

Stir spices into pancake mix, then add the molasses mixture just until moistened. Heat lightly oiled griddle or large nonstick skillet over medium heat. Pour pancakes on griddle and cook 4 to 5 minutes, turning once, until puffed and lightly browned. Serve with chunky cinnamon applesauce.

GINGER-SPICE WAFFLES

1 cup all-purpose flour
1 cup whole-wheat flour
2 tablespoons unsweetened cocoa powder
1 tablespoon ginger
1½ teaspoons baking soda
1½ teaspoons cinnamon
1 teaspoon nutmeg
½ teaspoon salt
2 eggs
1¾ cups buttermilk
¾ cup butter, melted
⅓ cup molasses
1½ cups low-fat vanilla yogurt
3 cups fruit, such as blueberries, chopped kiwi, and mandarin oranges

In a large bowl, sift together flour, whole-wheat flour, cocoa powder, ginger, baking soda, cinnamon, nutmeg, and salt. In a medium bowl, beat eggs slightly. Beat in buttermilk and butter until well blended. Make well in center of dry ingredients. Add buttermilk mixture and molasses to well; stir just until ingredients are combined and dry ingredients are moistened. Make 6 waffles in waffle maker following manufacturer's directions. Stack between sheets of waxed paper on large baking sheet and keep warm in 225-degree oven. Serve waffles topped with vanilla yogurt and fruit.

DID YOU KNOW?

Americans have always celebrated Christmas with gingerbread. Gingerbread houses were particularly popular in the nineteenth century—elaborate Victorian houses, heavy with candies and sugar icicles.

GINGERBREAD PUDDING

5 tart apples of your choice, quartered
½ cup sugar
1 teaspoon cinnamon
¼ teaspoon nutmeg
Pinch salt
½ cup water

Topping:
½ cup sugar
1 teaspoon cinnamon
1 teaspoon baking soda
½ cup molasses
1 cup boiling water
1 teaspoon ginger
½ cup butter
Flour

Preheat oven to 350 degrees. Fill a 2-quart baking dish half full of apples. Combine sugar, cinnamon, nutmeg, and salt; sprinkle over apples, then pour ½ cup water over all. For topping, mix together all ingredients, using enough flour to make a thick batter; spread over apples and bake 30 minutes.

GINGERBREAD-RAISIN SCONES

2 cups flour
1 tablespoon baking powder
¾ teaspoon cinnamon
½ teaspoon ginger
⅛ teaspoon cloves
⅓ cup dark brown sugar, packed
6 tablespoons chilled butter, cut into pieces

¼ cup milk
1 large egg
3 tablespoons light molasses
1 teaspoon vanilla
⅔ cup raisins

Preheat oven to 375 degrees. Lightly grease baking sheet. Blend first 6 ingredients in food processor. Add butter and process until mixture resembles coarse meal. In a large bowl, beat milk, egg, molasses, and vanilla. Add flour mixture and raisins; stir gently until dough forms. Gather dough into ball. On lightly floured surface, press dough into 1-inch-thick round. Cut round into 8 wedges. Place on prepared baking sheet. Bake until toothpick inserted into center comes out clean, about 25 minutes. Serve warm.

GINGER SUNDAE SAUCE

⅓ cup light corn syrup
¼ cup candied ginger, finely chopped
Dash salt
½ cup light cream, divided
¼ cup butter
½ teaspoon vanilla

In a small saucepan, mix together corn syrup, candied ginger, salt, and ¼ cup light cream. Simmer 5 minutes. Gradually stir in remaining light cream. Heat through, but do not boil. Remove from heat; stir in butter and vanilla. Serve warm over vanilla ice cream.

GINGER FRUIT FREEZE

3 ounces cream cheese, softened
3 tablespoons mayonnaise
1 tablespoon lemon juice
¼ teaspoon salt
½ cup preserved kumquats, chopped
½ cup dates, chopped
¼ cup maraschino cherries, quartered
1 (8¾ ounce) can crushed pineapple, drained
2 tablespoons candied ginger, finely chopped
1 cup whipped cream
½ cup toasted slivered almonds

In a large bowl, mix together cream cheese, mayonnaise, lemon juice, and salt. Stir in kumquats, dates, maraschino cherries, crushed pineapple, and candied ginger. Fold in whipped cream. Pour into 1-quart refrigerator tray. Sprinkle toasted slivered almonds over top. Freeze until firm. Makes 6 to 8 servings.

GINGERBREAD COFFEE CAKE

2⅓ cups cake flour
1 teaspoon salt
1 teaspoon baking soda
1 teaspoon ginger
½ teaspoon cloves
1½ teaspoons cinnamon

½ teaspoon allspice
1 cup butter, softened
1¼ cups brown sugar
2 eggs, beaten
⅔ cup cold strong coffee

Preheat oven to 375 degrees. Grease two 9-inch layer pans. In a small bowl, sift dry ingredients together 3 times. In a large bowl, cream butter and brown sugar until fluffy. Add eggs and beat well. Add flour alternately with coffee to butter/sugar mixture, beating after each addition. Turn into prepared pans. Bake 25 minutes.

BRAIDED GINGERBREAD

1 cup brown sugar, packed
3 eggs
1¼ cups molasses
1 cup butter, softened
1 tablespoon baking soda
1 teaspoon salt

3 cups flour, plus 5 to 6
    cups to be added later
1 teaspoon cinnamon
1 teaspoon ginger
1 teaspoon allspice

Early in the day or up to a week ahead, beat together all ingredients in a large bowl. Stir in additional 5 to 6 cups of flour to make a stiff dough. Divide dough in half and wrap in plastic; refrigerate at least 3 hours. Preheat oven to 350 degrees. Grease a baking sheet. Divide one-half of dough into 3 ropes approximately 1 inch thick and 12 inches long. Make ropes by rolling dough between the palms of your hands. Lay 3 ropes side by side on baking sheet. Pinch the tops of the 3 ropes together firmly. Braid the ropes and pinch the ends together firmly. Repeat with the other half of dough. Bake 20 minutes or until done. Remove from oven. Immediately brush with Lemon Glaze (see recipe on p.118) while braid is still warm.

LEMON GLAZE

2 tablespoons lemon juice
1 cup powdered sugar
Water

Mix lemon juice and powdered sugar. Add enough water to bring to the desired consistency.

DID YOU KNOW?

Gingerbread is an ancient treat. Egyptians were eating gingerbread when the great pyramid of Cheops was still young—but the first recipe came from Greece, where, in about 2400 BC, a baker from the island of Rhodes created it. The unleavened, honey-sweetened cakes became famous.

HIGH-ALTITUDE GINGERBREAD

2½ cups flour
¼ teaspoon baking soda
½ teaspoon salt
¼ teaspoon cinnamon
¼ teaspoon nutmeg
¼ teaspoon allspice

1 teaspoon ginger
½ cup soft shortening
½ cup sugar
2 eggs
¾ cup molasses
⅔ cup boiling water

Preheat oven to 350 degrees. Grease and flour a 9x9-inch pan. Sift together 3 times the following ingredients: flour, baking soda, salt, cinnamon, nutmeg, allspice, and ginger. In a separate bowl, cream together shortening and sugar. Add eggs, one at a time, beating well after each addition. Add molasses and mix thoroughly. Add dry ingredients to wet ingredients alternately with water. Beat about 20 strokes after each addition of flour and 30 strokes after each addition of liquid. Pour batter into pan. Bake 45 minutes.

WHEATLESS GINGERBREAD

1¼ cups rice flour
1¼ cups cornstarch
2 teaspoons baking soda
1 teaspoon cinnamon
¼ teaspoon cloves
¼ teaspoon ginger

½ cup sugar
1 cup molasses
½ cup butter, softened
1 cup boiling water
2 eggs, well beaten

Grease and flour a 9x9-inch pan. Sift together 6 times the following ingredients: rice flour, cornstarch, baking soda, cinnamon, cloves, and ginger. In a separate bowl, mix together sugar, molasses, butter, and boiling water. Add eggs and stir well. Combine all ingredients and beat until thoroughly mixed. Bake at 350 degrees for 45 minutes.

GINGERBREAD PUMPKIN CAKE

½ cup walnut halves
2 cups cake flour, sifted
4 teaspoons baking powder
1 teaspoon baking soda
¼ teaspoon salt
1½ teaspoons cinnamon
½ teaspoon ginger
¼ teaspoon nutmeg
1 cup plus 2 tablespoons brown sugar
3 large eggs, room temperature
¼ cup canola oil
3 tablespoons walnut oil, room temperature
1 teaspoon vanilla
1½ cups pumpkin puree

Preheat oven to 350 degrees. Grease and flour a 10-inch fluted metal tube pan. In a medium bowl, whisk walnut halves, flour, baking powder, baking soda, salt, cinnamon, ginger, and nutmeg. In a separate bowl, beat brown sugar, eggs, canola oil, and walnut oil on medium-high speed for 3 minutes. Beat in vanilla and pumpkin until just smooth. Add flour mixture; beat until completely moistened. Scrape batter into prepared pan. Bake 30 minutes or until toothpick inserted in center comes out clean. Let cake cool 10 minutes. Invert onto wire rack to cool completely.

PUMPKIN GINGERBREAD TRIFLE

2 (14 ounce) packages gingerbread mix
1 (6 ounce) box vanilla pudding mix (not instant)
1 (20 ounce) can pumpkin pie filling
½ cup brown sugar, packed
½ teaspoon cinnamon
¼ teaspoon ginger
1 (12 ounce) container frozen whipped topping

Bake gingerbread according to package directions. Cool completely. Prepare pudding according to package directions and set aside to cool. Stir pumpkin pie filling, brown sugar, cinnamon, and ginger into pudding. Crumble 1 batch of gingerbread into the bottom of a large trifle bowl. Pour half of pudding mixture over gingerbread. Add a layer of whipped topping. Repeat with the remaining gingerbread, pudding, and topping. Refrigerate overnight.

LEMON GINGERBREAD SQUARES

2 cups molasses
⅔ cup butter, softened
3 teaspoons baking soda
2 eggs, beaten
1 cup sour cream
4 cups flour
1 tablespoon ginger

1 tablespoon cinnamon
1 teaspoon salt
1 (6 ounce) package
  lemon pie pudding
  (not instant)

Preheat oven to 350 degrees. Grease a 9x13-inch pan. In a saucepan, combine molasses and butter. Heat to boiling point. Add soda and beat hard. Add eggs and sour cream. In a separate bowl, combine all dry ingredients. Add molasses mixture to dry ingredients. Blend well. Pour into pan. Bake 15 minutes. Prepare lemon pie pudding according to package directions. As soon as gingerbread is removed from oven, spread pudding evenly over the top of the warm gingerbread. Immediately put into refrigerator. Refrigerate at least 2 hours. Cut into squares. Serve chilled.

GINGERBREAD CAKE

1 cup molasses
¼ cup maple syrup
¾ cup butter
2 cups flour
1 teaspoon baking soda

1 teaspoon ginger
1 teaspoon cinnamon
½ teaspoon allspice
1 cup warm milk
2 eggs

Preheat oven to 325 degrees. Grease a 9x13-inch pan. In a saucepan, combine molasses, syrup, and butter; bring to a boil. In a large bowl, sift all dry ingredients. Add molasses mixture and warm milk. Stir well until smooth. Add eggs and blend thoroughly. Pour batter into pan. Bake 2 hours.

SOFT GINGERBREAD CAKE

1 cup butter, softened
1 cup sugar
2 tablespoons cinnamon
2½ tablespoons ginger
teaspoon nutmeg
¼ cup lemon juice

3 eggs
1 cup molasses
1 teaspoon baking soda
   dissolved in ½ cup   ¼
   hot water
2½ cups flour

Preheat oven to 350 degrees. Grease a 9x13-inch pan. In a large bowl, cream butter and sugar. Add spices, lemon juice, eggs, molasses, and soda in water. Beat on medium speed for 30 seconds. Add flour. Blend well. Pour batter into pan. Bake 30 minutes.

GRANDMOTHER'S GINGERBREAD CAKE

1 cup shortening
1 cup sugar
1 cup molasses
2 eggs, beaten
2 cups flour
1 teaspoon salt

1 tablespoon ginger
1 tablespoon cloves
1 teaspoon baking soda
1 tablespoon cinnamon
2 cups sour cream
1 cup raisins

Preheat oven to 325 degrees. Grease a loaf pan. In a large bowl, cream shortening and sugar. Add molasses and eggs. In a separate bowl, sift dry ingredients together. Add to sugar mixture alternately with sour cream. Add raisins last. Pour into loaf pan. Bake 1 hour.

ORANGE GINGERBREAD CAKE

5 eggs
1 cup sugar
1 cup butter, softened
1 cup molasses
2 teaspoons baking powder
1 cup milk

¼ cup orange juice
3½ cups sifted flour
1 teaspoon ginger
1 teaspoon cinnamon
1 teaspoon allspice
1 teaspoon salt

Preheat oven to 350 degrees. Grease a 9x13-inch pan. In a large bowl, beat eggs, sugar, and butter until light and fluffy. Add all other ingredients. Beat together until completely blended. Pour batter into pan. Bake 30 minutes or until done. Serve warm.

GINGERBREAD WITH
BANANA APRICOT GLAZE

2 cups molasses
⅔ cup butter, softened
3 teaspoons baking soda
2 eggs, beaten
1 cup sour cream
4 cups flour
1 tablespoon ginger
1 tablespoon cinnamon
1 teaspoon salt
3 bananas, sliced
2½ cups cooked apricots with juice
1 cup sugar
⅓ cup boiling water

Preheat oven to 350 degrees. Grease a 9x13-inch pan. In a saucepan, combine molasses and butter. Heat to boiling point. Add soda and beat hard. Add eggs and sour cream. In a separate bowl, combine flour, ginger, cinnamon, and salt. Add butter mixture to dry ingredients. Blend well. Pour into pan. Bake 15 minutes. When gingerbread is removed from oven, cover top with slices of banana until completely covered. In a saucepan over medium heat, cook apricots, sugar, and boiling water. Cook until thick like jam. Spread over warm gingerbread and bananas.

CREAM CHEESE GINGERBREAD

2 cups molasses
⅔ cup butter, softened
3 teaspoons baking soda
2 eggs, beaten
1 cup sour cream
4 cups flour
1 tablespoon ginger

1 tablespoon cinnamon
1 teaspoon salt
1 (8 ounce) package
    cream cheese, softened
2 tablespoons heavy
    cream

Preheat oven to 350 degrees. Grease a 9x13-inch pan. In a saucepan, combine molasses and butter. Heat to boiling point. Add soda and beat hard. Add eggs and sour cream. In a separate bowl, combine flour, ginger, cinnamon, and salt. Add butter mixture to dry ingredients. Blend well. Pour into pan. Bake 15 minutes. Cool completely. Beat together cream cheese and cream. Cut gingerbread into squares. Split squares and put cream cheese mixture between layers.

GINGERBREAD PARTY DESSERT

2 cups molasses
⅔ cup butter, softened
3 teaspoons baking soda
2 eggs, beaten
1 cup sour cream

4 cups flour
1 tablespoon ginger
1 tablespoon cinnamon
1 teaspoon salt

Preheat oven to 350 degrees. Grease a 9x13-inch pan. In a saucepan, combine molasses and butter. Heat to boiling point. Add soda and beat hard. Add eggs and sour cream. In a separate bowl, combine all dry ingredients. Add butter mixture to dry ingredients. Blend well. Pour into pan. Bake 15 minutes. When gingerbread is removed from oven, immediately top hot gingerbread with Orange Cream Cheese Topping (see recipe on p. 136).

BUTTERSCOTCH GINGERBREAD SQUARES

2 cups molasses
⅔ cup butter, softened
3 teaspoons baking soda
2 eggs, beaten
1 cup sour cream
4 cups flour
1 tablespoon ginger
1 tablespoon cinnamon
1 teaspoon salt
1 (12 ounce) package butterscotch morsels

Preheat oven to 350 degrees. Grease a 9x13-inch pan. In a saucepan, combine molasses and butter. Heat to boiling point. Add soda and beat hard. Add eggs and sour cream. In a separate bowl, combine flour, ginger, cinnamon, and salt. Add butter mixture to dry ingredients. Blend well. Pour into pan. Bake 15 minutes. Put butterscotch morsels in microwaveable bowl. Microwave in 30-second intervals until morsels are completely melted. As soon as gingerbread is removed from oven, spread melted butterscotch evenly over the top of the warm gingerbread. Immediately put into refrigerator. Refrigerate at least 2 hours. Cut into squares. Serve chilled.

ORANGE CREAM CHEESE TOPPING

6 ounces cream cheese
1¼ cups sifted powdered sugar
3 tablespoons orange juice
1 teaspoon lemon juice

Blend all ingredients until smooth. Spread onto Gingerbread Party Dessert (see recipe on p.133).

GINGERBREAD CRAFTS

New every year,
Newborn and newly dear,
He comes with tidings and a song,
The ages long, the ages long.

ALICE MEYNELL

GINGERBREAD COOKIE ORNAMENTS

½ cup butter, softened
½ cup dark brown sugar, loosely packed
½ cup molasses
3½ cups flour
1 teaspoon cinnamon
1 teaspoon ginger
½ teaspoon salt
¼ teaspoon cloves
1 teaspoon baking soda
⅓ cup water
Gingerbread Craft Icing (see recipe on p. 140)

In a large bowl, cream together butter and brown sugar. Add molasses and mix well. In a separate bowl, sift together dry ingredients. With mixer on low speed, slowly add dry ingredients and ⅓ cup water to molasses mixture. If dough gets too stiff, mix with your hands. Work dough with your hands until smooth. Turn out onto a piece of plastic wrap, form into a neat rectangle, wrap well, and refrigerate for at least 1 hour or overnight. Preheat oven to 350 degrees. Roll out dough to just under ¼-inch thickness. Cut out as many cookies as possible. Place cookies on parchment-lined baking sheets and bake for 10 to 15 minutes, or until firm. When the cookies are just out of the oven, use a bamboo or metal skewer to make a small hole ½ inch from the top of each one to accommodate a hook or cord. After cookies cool, spread a layer of icing on each one and decorate as desired with silver balls in assorted sizes. Reinsert skewers to keep holes open. To allow icing to set, leave cookies for 30 minutes in an oven on the lowest temperature.

GINGERBREAD CRAFT ICING

3½ cups powdered sugar
3 egg whites (If you plan to eat the house, use powdered egg whites.)

In a large bowl, beat powdered sugar and egg whites until smooth. Place in a pastry bag fitted with a small tip or in a large resealable plastic bag with a small piece cut off a bottom corner.

GINGERBREAD WREATH

Make Ginger Crisps dough (see recipe on p. 78); roll it out onto a well-floured work surface. Cut about 60 leaf shapes from the dough (use a couple of different cutters), and place the leaves on a parchment-lined baking sheet. Refrigerate until chilled, about 20 minutes. Using the back of a paring knife, press "vein" patterns into each leaf. Line another baking sheet with parchment paper. Using a dinner plate or cake pan as a template, draw an 8- or 9-inch circle on the paper. Place the leaves around the circle, brushing a bit of water with a pastry brush onto the back of each leaf before placing it over the next one. Overlap and stagger the leaves in the form of a wreath. Chill the wreath, about 20 minutes. Heat the oven to 350 degrees and bake the wreath until crisp but not darkened—12 to 15 minutes. Transfer wreath to a wire rack and let cool overnight. To decorate, sprinkle with powdered sugar put through a sieve. Ideally, the sugar on top of the gingerbread leaves will look like snowfall on real leaves. Attach a bow and hang away from heat or moisture.

EASIEST-EVER GINGERBREAD HOUSE

5 cups flour
2 teaspoon cinnamon
2 teaspoons ginger
½ teaspoon cloves
½ teaspoon baking soda
½ teaspoon salt

⅔ cup sugar
1 cup vegetable shortening
1 cup molasses
2 eggs
Gingerbread Craft Icing
(see recipe on p. 140)

Preheat oven to 350 degrees. Using cardboard or waxed paper, cut 1 pattern for each of the 4 walls. In a large bowl, combine flour, cinnamon, ginger, cloves, baking soda, and salt; mix well. In another large bowl, beat shortening and sugar until creamy. Add molasses and eggs; beat until well combined. Slowly stir in the flour mixture until a smooth dough forms. Divide the dough into 3 balls. Place 1 ball of dough on the back of a rimmed cookie sheet. Using a lightly floured rolling pin, roll out the dough to ⅛-inch thickness. Using the patterns and a sharp knife, cut out the front and back pieces; remove scraps from around the pieces and set aside. Bake pieces 10 to 12 minutes, or until lightly browned around the edges. Allow to cool slightly, then transfer to wire racks to cool completely. Repeat with another dough ball, cutting and baking the 2 side pieces. Repeat with the third dough ball, cutting and baking the 2 roof pieces. Form the scraps into a ball, roll out, and cut and bake the base piece. Assemble the house, using icing as glue.

To assemble the house:
Place the base, flat side down, in the center of a large platter or a piece of foil-wrapped cardboard. Lay the sides and front and back of the gingerbread house, flat side down, around the base. With the icing in a pastry bag or resealable plastic bag, pipe icing around the edges of each piece. Carefully lift and press the edges of the back piece and one side piece together, sealing with the icing. Lift the front piece and the remaining side piece and hold in place until the house is secure; let stand for a few minutes. Add additional icing to strengthen the joints. Place one roof piece in place. Pipe icing along the top inside edge of that piece and place the second roof piece in place. Pipe icing along all the seams of the house for extra support. Allow icing to dry and set at least 1 hour, preferably overnight, before decorating.

GINGERBREAD HOUSE DECORATING

Mini frosted shredded wheat cereal squares
Mini candy-coated chocolate pieces
Graham crackers
Gumdrops
Red and green mints
Peppermint sticks
Spearmint leaves
Red licorice laces
Jelly rings

To decorate:

The roof shingles are mini frosted shredded wheat cereal squares. Cover the roof with Gingerbread Craft Icing and attach the squares, frosted side up, in rows, overlapping them slightly. Make the chimney, windows, and doors out of graham crackers and secure them to the house with Gingerbread Craft Icing. Pipe icing icicles along the edge of the roof. Make bushes and wreaths from gumdrops—use spearmint leaves for the big bushes and jelly rings with mini candy-coated chocolate ornaments for the wreaths. Frame the windows and doors with peppermint sticks, licorice laces, and candy-coated chocolate pieces. Line mints along the top of the roof.

To make a snowy exterior:
For snow trees, place an ice cream cone upside down. With Gingerbread Craft Icing in a pastry bag or resealable plastic bag, pipe slightly overlapping rows of zigzags around the cone, starting from the bottom and ending at the top.

For a snowy landscape, sprinkle granulated sugar around the house and make footprints leading up to the door by making small indentations with the blunt end of a pencil or pen.

DID YOU KNOW?

Germany has a long tradition of producing flat, shaped gingerbreads. Fourteenth-century Germans formed gingerbread guilds and used carved molds to create gingerbread masterpieces for the aristocracy. German bakers in the 1600s were the first to add molasses to their recipes—and they were the ones who began the tradition of celebrating the holidays with gingerbread.

STAINED GLASS GINGERBREAD HOUSES

½ cup butter, softened
¾ cup sugar
1 egg
¼ cup dark molasses
3 cups flour
1 tablespoon pumpkin pie spice

2 teaspoons ginger
2 teaspoons vanilla
½ teaspoon salt
½ teaspoon baking soda
Hard candy of varying
    colors, crushed

In a large bowl, with an electric mixer on medium speed, beat butter until creamy. Add sugar, then beat in egg, molasses, flour, pumpkin pie spice, ginger, vanilla, salt, and soda. Preheat oven to 350 degrees. Lightly grease baking sheets. Roll out each piece of dough ¼- to ⅛-inch thickness. Cut out cookies with house-shaped cutters. Cut out windows with smaller star- and triangle-shaped cutters. (If dough becomes too soft, refrigerate until firm.) Place cookies on well-greased baking sheets and fill window holes with different colored crushed hard candies. Bake 8 to 12 minutes. Cool on sheets until candy in windows has set; transfer to wire rack and cool completely. Outline the houses and windows with Gingerbread Craft Icing (see recipe on p. 140).

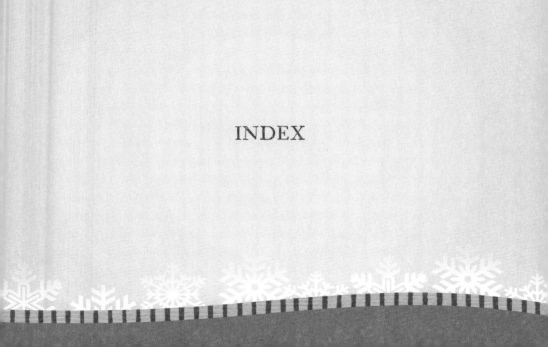

INDEX